A THOUSAND CURVES

PAUL NEMSER

ISBN 978-1-952204-11-1
Printed in the United States of America

RED MOUNTAIN PRESS

Santa Fe, New Mexico
www.redmountainpress.us

For Rebecca

CONTENTS

AFTER THE CALM

Our furniture is turning to nails' ends and cows' ears.
We've stored no provisions for molasses-less times.
Used-up, riled-up hives—our hearts.
Pancakes burning in old butter—our backs.

On the bus ride after the geriatrician,
we smell angels powdering the breezes with lavender
and sit down to dream, and lie down to wake
and wake to read the split nutshells in our pockets—

to predict that a sheep will dance with weevils,
and a salmon lay down with a leaning willow—
thinking someone always wants
the rides nobody wants, which breaks our calm.

Bus-music jostles us, like changing tide
where islands once appeared upside down in the harbor,
and the loudest movement was a clam dropped on rocks,
a shard-splatter, a ganglion.

Bus crunches branch. We seize up. We sway.
I cradle your knuckles, as in olden days,
when we dipped a few fingers in wine.
We brushed only each other's lips,

crooned only songs titled, "I will"
for hours, in a field momentarily green.
I will. I will survive. I will rise. I will follow.
I will be. I will wait—for you.

Honey, wake up, you say, kneeing my hip
and smelling of eucalyptus. I love your eyes,
especially when we're shaken, flickering in glass, in weaves
of raspberries that thorn across fences fallen to gaps.

The bus lets us off near a panic of birds
who pluck the fall-aparts rotting red. Beaks veer drunk
into a rising cloud, and we get silly and scream
like wing-ier species that tear prey to bubbling violet:

"O goddess of raspberries, grant us red hands!"
Shrieks, chucks, pipes— where from? Lilt of songbirds
in a social praxis? In the frantic, dizzily companionable
wane of this day neither still nor sweet.

END OF THE CENTURY

We've slept too long, that hasn't stopped
the incidental warping, constellations
crossing, new diamond-scratch on glass.
Radio jumps off the nightstand, as the Ramones hammer
in the background their future, our present alarm.

You were a Japanese print of stars before blocks of wood,
a second of parallax before ticks were biting.
I love the short form of you, though no one keeps
time anymore, no one can say whose clouds
have stolen the stellar normal curves. Darling,

I remember now. I was supposed to report
on goats and goat paths in Eden. To trace wrens' flitting
at the motionless peripheries. To stop
the briefest minute as it shrinks like a tide.
I have known so much less than awareness asked of me.

Seaweed in the astral sea looks everywhere
to find the light. A lovely, lamented oil slick
rocks at star-set. The Great Bear will soon
bash a bird feeder off its pole,
bursting a supernova of sunflower seeds.

Nothing arrives as gears and maps predict. Nothing rings
bright or smooth. I was supposed to report
that the universe is kinked, resistance
is the lark song that estranges us from C,
there isn't any scratch we could call a note.

I was supposed to record a tuna's blue thrashing
in the foam of a soundless television storm.
Wasps fly at our teeth but miss and freak the screen.
It is beautiful to hear the sparks before we see them
in a window—in the window, our window-selves.

FOR AN ASTRONOMER'S DAUGHTER

Before this world,
                 we passed through clouds of others.

A world's hand stopped, as if still holding
                 a dropped phone.

Starry flourishes that can't be read when we look toward them,
                 that don't see us when we look away.

Slopes of pumice underfoot, and pumice in air scraping lips
                 down to first and last wishes.

Worlds in which I looked for you
                 and worlds in which I drank from you.

Middens of matter, a dense nothingness in them,
                 and spectra that luster along mothers-of-pearl.

Worlds of eye-deep islands in a coffee cup.
Shore-shimmer   shining   so many ways.
Broken liquid worlds that say, *Bring water in your hands.*

Bays torn white by a turbulence of dolphins,
                 bays torn blue by the two-hooked moon.

Dust of horizons crossed, billow-mist passed under.

What I call to you in this world I must
                 recall from some other.

Light gives a little shudder
                 just before I say your name.

A Donkey Duet In Val D'Orcia

Every morning we say it long and slow
like a nuzzle up the small wings of a spine.
By day we sound morning espresso.
At night a jeroboam of wine.

We hitch and squeak. It could be oak on oak,
or slaps on the nose for going forward on Whoa,
or backs loaded with stones to pack up the steps,
or just, *What have I done to you?*

Breathe in like screws turned in olive wood.
Sigh out like milk-happy foals.

Some days we don't have legs enough to plod these hills.
Other days it's her and him, and haw,
fueled by meadow hay and barley straw.

We wheeze like broken motor bikes.
Eyes flee to the sides of the head.
Ears V like old-time antennas.
We don't know what we've said.

We trust in noise. A door no one has oiled.
Tire on a broken axle. Shocksprings uncoiled.
We trust midges, zephyrs, nubs and stubs,
whooper swans and homer squabs.
Fencepost to fencepost, we run by twos,
and this pen becomes a temple to the honking muse.

Sometimes love and lovers, all creatures of a day,
palaver in a flawless, barnyard way,
and every hoofed life gets loudly foolish at a lope
in the morning beneath the smoggy slope.

In spring, you sing, you brayed for me
by the not-yet-weeping willow tree.
Along the vineyard's edge, at the valley's verge,
calls meet up near the loud river bridge.

Windows of white stucco houses shake.
Then farmers on featherbeds roll awake
and reach for each other, driven almost mad
by the long-held notes of donkeys
in a vale below the high pilgrim road.

AUBADE

We wanted nothing but hearts. To be hearts purely,
mounted on the knobs of perfect onyx backbones
lain in onyx cubes in the Museum of Hearts.

Or drifting through the Archipelago of Hearts—
oyster nights, oil-glint cities, shelves of sea.
We scribbled letters to our hearts inside cabinet drawers,

on the insides of a nautilus, on bubble chains left by a keel.
We talked of fish bones crushed and added to a life
like exotic salts, and the night-blue bouts of spring wind

that skim down and swat at shearwaters.
As if everything that matters were remembered
from a darkness out-darkened by a fire.

Wake with me. Let your voice bubble up
like nymphs in a bay
where women chew on snails

to stain their lips before they sing,
and wailing dogs no longer make their reputations
by snapping off the wings of wasps.

Yes, I'm brutal as a boat. I dip. I loop,
an old hull propelled by contrapuntal valves,
along built rivers under black bridges.

You're bird-frantic on a needly branch
out above the waves as they come in beating
at riverbanks where the moorings feel the sea.

Different heart-wrecks, palpitations.
Here they are, a wild red mash of crusts and ash.
Won't everything be thrown fire-first into the day?

For now, a gray machine is driving waves and sky.
Dockworkers pull the morning moon up by her arms
to watch her slither on carts, or dive to sea and swim away.

AUBADE WITH BEARS

Let me tickle your ear with a gentian bud.
It's dawn, purple and pursed in the mouth,
and we no longer wake up wild as bears at five,

crashing bird feeders and snouting on
to vacuum high bushes of their blueberries.
Isn't dawn the very best thing alive?

We were vaster once. We used up all the air—
my bellowing, your bugling. But now
mouth to mouth, we are medics, we revive.

MORNING

The wall plug sends runners vining through appliances,
and everything is charged by morning.

Ella sings, *What is this thing?* The crock pot is possessed.
Sleep is boiling like tomatoes. Darkness
cooks down. We wake— the reduction is day.

You put your nose into a glass of orange blossoms.
We hand it back and forth like a California
tinged with haze of smoke and oracles.

And why hide from tears, O earthlings born American?

On pea-green lawns aren't the For Sale signs
pure, instinctive, more-than-hypothetical?
But the songbook is ours, tunes never quite the same.

Every *goodnight*, we die a little.
Every day, sun saves our lives.

MORNING AFTER

All night I've run scaring rats through my insomnia.
They've climbed each other's rat backs and jumped into the sea.

Now you say, "The bed's a bivalve. It opens for us like wings."
You're better than the sunlight spotting things.

My pale, my pearl, my onions in a pan,
my gravity, my dew on the rise, my cyclone in a well—

"Don't worry," you say, and I hear, who can barely hear,
"We're just putting ourselves back in the oyster shell."

FUNCTIONARY

Counting drives me mad. Tabulations, eggs in a dozen-box,
how many boxes, how many folds.
Too much contained in too many containers.
Excess occupations. And time:

Sink-spouts; car-sputter; woodpeckers pecking;
air passing atoms under the door.
Diffused obsessions. Dead immortals.
A stone's skips in brooks, the propagating ripples.

I even count the times I have sailed beyond
my body only to wake in a parallel world.
That's where I meet you in the long night,
round a corner by a wall where all goes to infinity.

I say at the edge of a numberless reality.
"My angel, my dream," and we're bigger than the moon.
But back in this world, the census goes on,
and I'm wearing my uniform, fingers in gloves,

taking inventory on a coffee-stained ledger.
I hide from my boss, and her supervisor.
Everything I count is the opposite of true:
Not-you; not-you. Not one you.

IF I DON'T SEE YOU

I'll feel hollow as a blackbird
After the mariachis

I've had a crazy busy
Let's not finish anything

Let's flash into our phones
And like each other's cheekbones

I—how PDFs work
You—why a paralegal

We'll speak like it's curated
Overhear each other's hearts

And that's how we'll live
Like angels in an angel tree

My apartment's insanely cheap
Red ants and bluebottles

I'll die if you don't come here
I'll die after the mariachis

Then it has to be after
Hear—mariachis

I have lots of IDs
We could fly

BORDER

A girl who slept in a truck tire
and walked a year of miles
was driven back down through dry forests
on a small-eyed bus with drooping heads—
to no rooms for a child, but the murderers were there,
ones with fingers, ones with lips,
the spiny-back lizard who killed her brother
after Mama ran away
like an angel without wings.
I mean to find your father—did the girl
have a father? — *in America.*

That girl who slept in a truck tire,
whose brother was alive—she saw him
near the iron-slab graves,
where metal cattle sprawled in the yard.
The murderers tried
to hold the boy down. To squeeze
his brow, drink eyes for juice,
mix ears in a cup with clear liquor.
She snuck him away to the long roads.
The little box he carried in a sack--
he said it was his bones.

She lifted him with two hands,
pushed him with one.
Thousands of miles, he hung on her back.
Thousands more, he followed her.
They slept one night in an arc of tread.
When she woke, the dark-green
trees smelled of tar. She lost all the food.
They ate the long red grass,
until they felt like rats, until a few men saw.
Caught the boy, but the girl could run

until there were no train tracks,
pine-pitch, sun. And the moon
hung, a pitted blade,
above the floodlights.

20

She carved out a dark
that hid her from the guards.
She fooled the dogs because she smelled like rubber.

She fooled the wild pigs
because she smelled like a child.
She got up from a day in her truck tire
and by night crossed the border again.

LANDSCAPE WITH VIEW OF LAWYER

I press up near the big window
on the 19th floor,
like someone who cannot
make out much in a face,
but must go up to it
and squint close, run fingertips
over the cheeks, to be sure
of its shape,

though my desk
has disappeared
under the nimbus
and the precedents,

and every dawn I dream
I am a ritual slaughterer—
an honest, kind, and upright man—
with a knife, a whetstone,
and these teeth.

What I Knew And What I Had To Say

Dad didn't believe in speaking
before you had to speak.

Mom talked like a rainstorm
to keep stray planets away.

I remember struggles
with what I had to say.

On the Seaside Prom,
I'd run to a bench
and let my grandparents
catch up to me,

Grandma and Grandpa
with canes, colliding,
in and out of breath,
but they kept on talking

like their tongues were ponies
ahead of the Cossacks
whose braided whips were gaining.

It was fast, in Yiddish.
I didn't know
how they kept on.

And Mom and Dad,
a ways in front.
I thought she was a seagull,
flapping and lighting.

Him cormorant-grunting,
sometimes nodding,
or staring out toward
the insistence of the sea.

The whole conversation
out of earshot to me.

Then a beach fog that blew in
close around my arms
clung soft as wet fleece,
and flickered flames.

I thought the ocean
had wrapped me
in its tongues—

mouth of the Necanicum,
Tillamook Head,
the long winds
that gusted words
off white, drumming waves.

I didn't speak then,
I didn't know the way:

Here are my feet,
like a monkey's
on a man.

Here the mouth of a boy
learning where to stand,
who just learned to say

Here I am.

MITTE

By the time the company reconfigured the work plan, I was too old to use any of my skills. But I went along looking for another pile of trinkets, figuring my pockets were hardly full.
When we got to Berlin, the streets were so torn up that the night was a stumble through a coal pit, the holes leading only to holes. I fumbled to repair an underground switch, which, no matter what you pushed, snapped every light on, like some harsh accuser who cannot remember what you did, but knows you were the worst man in Germany.

There was no fixing the light, but I told folks I might have, and though pasts come back, memories might change.
My trip report is most accurate listing what I didn't see, like the World War II bomb they defused at the main train station while repelling my taxi into long, looping detours. I fell asleep once, crossing blocks of dotted-line borders, but I remembered the whole thing.

Section 3: "Missing at the Pergamon Altar—a giant's neck trampled by a sandaled foot, a tensely twisted seagod's gut, the heart-crushing way I was once in love with a headless goddess on a legless horse."

By the time I'd written this, I had nothing left. A balloon brushed my nose where I slumped in the park. I cried over babies while grinning like a grate and stared at a cart with glassed-in cheese. Construction was quiet; it must be Sunday. They brought me a hunk of grass frozen together like a bouquet and said: perhaps your family once lived here.

BOOKKEEPER

My hair, a new-poured copper.
In my wedding dress, a tulip in a narrow, fluted vase.
But beauty is a swift, flown.

My son came out of me willing as a cloud,
To me—a digit-starer,
shepherdess of integers, rebbetzin of ledgers.
I keep them blade-clean.

Heaven does not love wrong numbers.
Some days the books are angry enough
to tear the throat out of a bullock.
My desk smells of knife-wounds and razing.

I make an error. I fix it.

I teach my son to alphabetize.
He builds Jerusalems
of ordered papers. A stray sheet sails
to the streaky floor, like a seabird lighting
on salt that drawls with bubbles.
We pour ourselves, forget ourselves.
We count and lose count.
I tell him heaven is listening.

We eat our tuna on dark.

He practices sums, reading story problems
I've written on a paper.
Two, he says, *plus five,* he says. He looks up:
Is it listening now?

SONG OVER SONG FOR MY FATHER

Gotta go. Your tongue's all slurs.
The johnnie's a page of piss.
Lips cracking up. Hum setting fires.
Behold, letters fly, and only the parchment burns.
Fingers flutter. A tumult of wrens returns.
Chitters drown the radio jazz.
You ask me to bend your knees.
You tap slower than slow behind the beat.
A painted tent folds up into your eyes.
The animals no longer need the air, you say,
as I am breathing there
and start a prayer too late.

TIME SHARE

Mornings before Mom woke up dying
back at the time share,
before any of us knew
she was giving in at last, bones
about to break like crazy,
her blood eating up the rest of her,

Dad scuffed barefoot
dawn after dawn
to the brown foam-edge
of the brown-rice reef
and snapped the shutter
of his big handheld, the size
of our squirming 3-month old.

From where he stood, the angle
maybe didn't much matter,
but he knelt down, twisting,
        knees to water,
to make the long waves stand still
against the all-at-once
of some red everything.

Years later when he and
all his wives
were gone, I found packets,
hundreds of photos—
pure, preserved time—
in envelopes marked *Hawaii Sunrise*.

Stowed in a side drawer
of his home-office desk,
no dates on them.

Near-Sonnet With Homunculus

I was born with a baby on my tongue.
He liked the Milky Way, especially in mists.
He liked robots' coded conversations.
We could talk slower than a wagon pulled by ants,
or swift as spaghetti drawn in and down. Till he said,
"Goodbye my friend, my faithful vessel."
When I saw the gratitude in his aqua-blue eyes,
they turned to rivers deep enough for a small submarine.

He never showed himself to me again,
not even in the breath on a pocket mirror.
But sometimes my room puts on its own thick sleeve,
and the waters of life make an island of the day.
Sleeping at my desk, I hear gears deep down
and the low spin of his propeller.

QUESTIONS AT THE DROP-OFF

When I forget the sun sweeping by, windshield water creeping,
I start to believe in fixed stars, desert-clear, as might have been
before the Pole Star veered and we were always traveling.

But in this universe of pavement, zigzagging, lost,
your train soon to leave and we're stalled in exhaust,
the ground's a thousand holes, the air's wet dust
that floods my eyeballs, grits my watch.
The rain streaks and the map don't match.

You lug your bag. I reach out your guitar.
The ramp is slick as a clamshell. I slide back into my car.
Nothing's fixed. I turn the key, everything cracks
                    unendingly.

The wall-edges of downtown with its domes and folds
re-bend in a newer gravity. Light coalesces as a road,
the road as constellation. Fathers clutch across a gap,
and sons lean back again. We're tangent now, but then,
separated by cars under shifting, sighted stars.

I look out for your eyes, clocks rush toward noon.
Will you be back tomorrow?
            "See you later."   "See you soon."

A WAY TO THE NORTH

The future was a smear on the map of the pole,
but the wagons did not stop coming.
They were loaded with grain and cornhusks,
fish wearing beards of ice.
They carted apples the color of pinpricks,
and timber still trembling from its fall.
The road wound so long, through country so harsh
that any softness of a cloud about to thunder
was wool of a new-shorn lamb;
the muted violence of rapids from afar
was the murmuring of lungs.
Farmers had to argue long, like a fever
that seared the forehead, bubbled the eyes
till the last wheatberry dried to a ghost
under cloud stretched
to hints and whispers.
Much was forgotten, and the rest was chaff.
The rest was a rising of wind in ears,
a scent of red mushrooms.
Everyone dreaming of shocked light,
transformations of the troubled heart,
and breadless breakfasts as the earth revolves,
till that edgy shaky earthquake of a day
when they faced north,
and north was an enemy.
"Don't touch me, cold one,"
they said among the pines
above the frozen feet of the frozen wisps
that were smoke when the world was new.
That was when I saw you,
on foot and winded as an angel
who began by a palm in a dry moment,
the smear of pistachio crushed in your eyes.
Dates on your lips, you glided my way,
in sealskin and cradling a zither.
Black lambswool hair, and spidery hands,
and you strummed,
and we leapt without slipping.

BLESSING OVER WATER

First, I learned there is no blessing over water,
but there is—

By your word, all has come to be.

To be pale falls of spray, sung most at a precipice.
To drink in, as when snow-gray geese
look down. Wave breaks to waves,
I look out towards the vortex, listen down
through fog, swallowing drops
as scarp gives to slide. Whatever railing keeps me
at the edge, I hold onto it.
Water wetting lips, mist saying sky.

MOTIVATION [DELUGE]

The scene: whitecaps eat their babies.

All the boat can see—
what a foolish, lovable sleep we're born to.
All it can hear—black whales battering,
squeals of wet-rot, thuds of hull.

Whose wind?

The boat rides a horse
which bucks the boat's brains
to a soup and spills them.

The ocean is a sun-fire of jellies.

Fish entrails, briny wool, sea lettuce,
salt that will never come out of my hair—

Rain drapes the deck with gray curtains.

No matter whose wind,
I'll beach us where land is long,
and the tiny fruits on twigs grow into birds.

THE ORIGIN OF YET

The Origin of Yet Has Been an Object of Endless Speculation
An Analytic Dictionary of English Etymology— Anatoly Liberman

One day the rain may make us blind—mollusk shells
that walk about without the flesh, without a lens.
Hard-ribbed curvatures looking to find hands
under the very sameness of the sky we daily drown in.
The uncondemned houses never reach this far.
We can almost taste the seaweed on the sea.
You beat and beat a little foot. Everything
is gentle as after a hurricane. O eyes that look into
the distance and know what's coming!
Some days we're lion-toothed, some we're not even rabid.
We flutter like finches that crack on the tongue.
Or we imitate beetle legs without the beetle body,
walking in rhythm along the window, out a screen hole
with a pure insistent thrum. Come shelter
under this apple in flower, its pink ohs opening.
How did it learn to be so kind? For moments,
we're out of danger, afraid of nothing—when
a rain that had never rained begins to rain.

VIEW FROM A BLIND

Behind tree-branch traceries,
green tea steaming in a thermos, we hide.

The pause is getting to you.

Will there be wings, fish jumps?
Morning star blinking in a trance of ripples?

What would a Cassandra have said
if she had seen
the geese in ruins?

Shouts from other blinds,
shots from seeping clouds,
a torment of birds
falling out of their feathers.

Winds fade barely loud
as last-year's raven songs.

You fling your eyes out through the blockage
toward bird bones and fire.

Never far from joy—you.

A gray-winged cortex
that collides with a wave,
another wave-splash—I.

We are geese. You run to fly.

No, no, we'll plunge out of the sky,
zero and zero to wave tops to the end.

Then I forget about all that,
and I run after you.

CURRENT

Oars spoon light through a bank-less river.
Tree wings furl upward higher than birds.
This air this weave this me now to you
sky a nerve net sparking blue.

We're contortionists on a river float.
You paddle with your first and second toes.
I with my deviated nose. We fixate
on bubble streams crashing off the boat.

Pitiless gravelly going-down sun
throws its voice through the vaulted dome.
A chilling wind tears holes in my skin.
Fish scales mirror falling stars.

What's the grammar for travels to come?
No snoring no commas no fir-needle strumming
no microbe squirming no cricket scratch. No.
No saving no grace for mirages of day?

What will happen you say and say.
You untwist the water bottles—
heavy with hope—and drink almost to drowning.
Maybe we need to pray how to pray

light comes full alive and the stream tells us who
will watch waves on their seafaring way.
Leapers down ladders young salmon will say
when their fins comb kelp in the bay.

CITYSCAPE

And what if we once had more than this green water?
This dust obliterating toothy, towered roofs?
What was it like before they de-loused the bookstores,
before they dumped the developer fluid from darkrooms?

I'm full of fluid now. Some I've drunk,
some's burst from cells. Yet my nose finds lovely
this purple nightmare of a rot, when grapes
creep along dark arbors of X'd out memory.

So grand this nest of telephone wire and clothesline
spit messages at me like wine at a wall.
You were barefoot and soft-palmed, I'm sure you were,
before they shot all the wild dogs by the big box store.

IN THE ALLEY OF PERPETUAL INDUSTRY

Full of thrown cans and bins, it smells like mammals.
Rain insinuates into wood. A puddle trembles
like a vat of black vinyl fish.
Falls of sour milk, sour melon.
Congealed balls of motor oil.
A yellowed technical manual has a crust
of dried honey and insect mandibles.

There are spirits in this world
from worlds already mouldering.
They come strong and sharp as smoke
or like apples and their peelings
going bad but still sweet
after the starlings have been at them
and they stick to our shoes.

Everything sticks to our shoes
where new manufactories will decompose it all—
a feather mattress thick with comings-to;
bassoonings, hisses, corpses, cruds.
Our lips and eyelids burn away,
leaving all we crack open for holy,
all we mistake for decay.

BIRTHDAY AND CENTIPEDE

Air has never felt so green. The park's
a mesh of bracken. A peach in the street weeps
       pearls from a bruise.
Is it possible to take too many steps
into the mystery? And why
should why not melt me down?

Why should the sun not be brighter
than any that blinded me before?

Life wild and eager swarms through the leaf litter.
No shortness of breath, or shortness of breathlessness.
       Every single segment takes and gives out air.
They have so many legs—they run down a drainpipe,
and a few of them think they're still above ground!

On streets where black vinyl flaps and cracks,
a sprawling spirea flutters veils.
Minutes ago they were shredded gray gauze,
and it melts me. Melts me down.

(So somebody climbs into my ear today
and tells me to dance with my forerunners,
slithers, and stumbles, and no-damns-given climbs,
while a billion mouths, deep in the shitpiles,
break the old days down.)

DRISHTI

And my mouth overflowed with yogurt and minted honey.
But then a future came:

trees falling on street corners and on the schools,
salmon-crushing trees in heavy seas.

Postures of dislocation, despair, immolation.
The burning of bonds to free my heart into the air,
a red powder and a blue and a yellow.

Mazes made from the flight of sparrows
out of sharp, falling branches.

I counted backward through the rooms of the tall building
where daily I'd skittered, hoarding and lizarding.

I removed my neck from the subway tracks
because the train was never coming because the tunnels
overflowed—milk and slow nectars had swallowed the wheels—

and I could see beyond the platform the trees on fire
that broke open the windows, the order
of things—trunk halves, root casings, phloem.

And a rain ran wild with open eyes.

WITHOUT A WHISPER

The people carried a homeland in their pockets,
for the world was infested with matter.
A straw house could be midwife to a bonfire.
The old stories left the people cold.
It wasn't safe to rely too much on anyone.
Anyone might die without a whisper.

Of course, an idol might scare a ravening brigand;
its worship was worth bouquets.
Burn goat bones, lie in egg yolk,
chew cured hearts. It wouldn't serve
in place of gruel. Wouldn't tame a loud, mad dog.
Anyone might die without a whisper.

The wise man understood that the people longed
for spectacle—as if his staff were the lever
that would move ten mountains,
and his tent were the wing
that would soar above green fields
after they had died without a whisper.

The wise knew that matter was a dangerous thing.
They were experts in diplomacy.
They spoke of God
as a next best friend,
unashamed of their ancient simplicity.
They too might die without a whisper.

MY AUNT REMEMBERS

Whose desire, Mama, drove a fiddle like a bird
thinking only of beautiful claws?
Papa, who made arks of baling wire and balsa
and tied up the Yiddish books and saved them
from the dentures, when death was too young
to sleep soundly, and life was too old to shine shoes?
I mean there was a barber shop in the oldest part of town
where the men had no hair, and the women
slept alone. There was a dress shop for polka dots,
and a tailor for holes. And the singing!
Like lights going out at 7, the calm
of a weather that is rain and rain, and the rain
steams up on the inside of the houses, and the kids
are made of baling wire and balsa.
There's nothing to worry about, and all the prophets
have whales. I am certain there was a fireplace.
I am sure there was morning. And stories
about eggplant and chicken feet and pletzlach
before the innocent were old, and the innocent
were drunken, and the innocent were tried
for being innocent again—ladle after ladle, they were tried.
For this reason, death came in its black trombovke.
It came one day, and it came another,
and scolded you to drive memory's wagon with whips.
You beat the nag with bags of carrots
until Papa had twisted enough wire to make an ark,
and all the sweet yesterdays wickered—
yes, we'll board—but the angry ones
climbed rock piles pretending to be goats.
They wound me a wig of goats' hair,
and chased me home, biting my back
because you were my Mama, because you'd know
their braided hats by the curved holes for horns.
You had a bowlful of currants. Can't you
remember? How they swallowed our eyes
when red currants touched our tongues?

Meeting You After Chernobyl

The last frozen day had come and gone, and we were
sleeping in the elbows of trees in the elbow of a town,
our sutures all sunken together as if we shared one wound,
as if we had climbed from a single pit

like a race of dinosaurs grown from a fused lump of eggs
that had slept in valley ice for three shifts in the North Star,
as the leaves undecorated the last few branches,
which were skinny as bat bones

There were cattle blotched with waning alphabets,
and eyes that had seen too many lights,
so we didn't recognize the wells
we had drunk from all our lives, nor

the creek that flowed with clothes and flesh,
nor the seeds brought from all over the countryside,
from knifed sacks in waterlogged barns, from pods
trembling on grotesque grasses.

We talked to each other until we could not talk.
It was gobbledygook, was joy, nothing to remember:
We would not be overrun like ants by a larger horde of ants.
The darkness would not come closer.

A dog would lift its howl to where the wind left
the tablecloths—crumpled, clawed up, drying in the sun.
A phalanx of trucks that had jostled our vertebrae
would sound like bubbles in a bottle.

I never missed you so much as waking from that sleep.
I dream of you now lingering barely below ground,
all your twenty fingers warbling together as on flutes.
My pores open to you as to rain.

Years give way to lakes of white dust to unyielding dirt-land.
The snouts of oxen stain pale as marble
when the beasts haul blades through the hardness that remains
of what decades ago had been garden.

STARS THAT NEVER TOUCH THE SEA

Though I live far away on the shores of Scythia, with those stars visible that never touch the sea. . .. —Ovid, *Tristia*

The beaches are hemmed in with sea lavender, and the smell
oh the smell of clams undermines me. Memory,
I have none at all, though the streets were never wetter.

I come up to the seawall, and the living are sad
as a soldier who halts of his own accord, not even turning an ear
for the command, but stopping because there is too much rain

or because a girl will not stop weeping.
She sits on a stone adding consonants to tears
like celery stalks to a stew with no beef

but only the thrice-boiled bones so white
they turn cheeks into moon-white halos of ice, and the soldier
traces the nerves in her face, as if she were the melting moon.

I've fallen out of myself like a gear out of a gear train.
I peel back fir cones, artichoke-style,
stare horrified at beetles. Do legs have to twitch?

Like every straw in a straw pile, I pick teeth for foreign bodies—
amoebas, angels, the sixteenth notes
that shudder a creature's mandibles.

Everyone mmmm's through the daily carnage.
The geese are a full battalion in battle dress.
Sand is a yellow shelf of weepers and fleshpickers.

Dancing for all who didn't slaughter me in effigy,
I stick like gum in the day's golden hair
while a dog's eyes are squeezing all the blue from a cloud,

and hours are swooped up by barn swallows.
Hours with the experienced, vacant look
that saddens around the stare of a warhorse.

Are flowers the ditties of the foolish and forsaken?
Dragonfly tongue, lie in wait behind my smile.
Suppositions of bees, rub me in pollen,

I'm a man with a beard. A squint by the seaside
where day dried a mountain of pale pink salt
in the light of this woman's moaning song.

LETTER FROM BERLIN

Stones block other stones.
The buildings—headlines.

Clouds of people—
are they people again?

Still icy here. Glass
breaks, gives back the street.

Black-skid taxis by the embassies,
the Tiergarten.

Chimpanzees whoop for apples
thrown into their enclosure.

Next morning through the hotel's
breakfast room window,
I see ostriches,

reed-necked male fluffing and rocking
behind the quiet female,
their hot, individual breaths.

All April first I've dreamt and redreamt
that everyone's feet are asleep,
strange to spring snow,

trudging through peaceful-frantic-
shaded-by-cranes-placing-I-beams

gardens.

What can't be undone?
said the night builders,

waking me before there were birds,
the first
a nightingale.

MIL CUMBRES

After the sagging colonial square
came facades piled with columns of tires
and a man's eyes the color of dried grass.

I pulled over to ask for the right road.
"Every road leads to the capital, and none
of the roads is good. Follow to the north,

you'll see the way, but whatever you do, what-
ever you do, do not take the road to Mil Cumbres."
We drove, by roads marked north, wound through hills

with dark-green forest verging,
Gray fingers drifted in from left and right,
a mist wetter than rain. As the car climbed,

road slid in and out of view, then
down-spirals rolled us like dice out of a cup,
threw us back in, and rolled us,

till the pavement spiraled up again.
Once, I pulled over onto a pine-heavy shoulder.
A sign showed a foot stepping off a cliff.

An hour more, a bus came head-on for us. I swerved,
one tire hung over the ravine,
and yellow butterflies flew up—torn paper.

Haze of a city far below, glints off tiny trucks
on roads dug out of outcrops, glimpses of drivers coiling
through crowds of igneous hills.

"Was there a number for this road?"
"What did he mean—Mil Cumbres?"
We looked it up: a thousand peaks, a thousand curves.

There were so many crescent moons that night,
moons that sang to no one,
or sang to hills' pine-tarred ears alone.

There was no way down.

FELICIDADE

"Sol vai se perder no mar."
—Teresa Cristina, "Acalanto"

I've heard that life begins
as a virus,
ends as a wedding
of methane rings,

that life is naked
giant otters at night.
But then—nichts
say the crickets. That's
what I've heard.

So I hold and hold
the crab of my heart.

I move one old leg
till it's my other leg.

I samba, and you samba.
You samba.
So do I.

I've heard that a back and forth
could teach sweet anything.

And we step. We step
into the anything that's here.

By a wet branch draped
in bird-beak orchids,
the waves are always saying,
We could. We could.

＊

We could finish 1000's
of sentences before love ended.
We could tie down ocean
by 1000's of little knots,
before it throws us on our backs,
before we rest in Yemanjá.

She shifts on the beach
in blue, rippling skirts
among all the fish with legs
who came out of her loins
to praise her with clear combs
and pearly bubbles.

Lie down, she says,
The waves are drums.

We've heard them
crossing the steamy bay
when the beaches
are almost opaline
and the sun above
the gas cracker plant
is high in the hydrocarbons.

Let's lie down. Here.
Until we die, and after

a small, unspeakable
shoal of chances of drowning

in joy.

FEBBRE A FEBBRAIO

Do not pare your nails too far back.
You will need them to peel back
the tape on your arm. That arm

is a map of the sewer system of Rome.
Until recently, your head was the biggest building
in the world: lion hotels, pilgrimage sites.

Even now, all your energy goes to clean
after vandals. You brush off
the chipped mosaic.

Just enough tiles—you can
make out the blue shoulder of a goddess
whose grace may yet take you by the elbow

to a stand of pine that drizzles into raw earth
bringing to life the taste of pitch.
Look at her: she is a sky that knows you perfectly—

deliverer of ice chipped from an Alp,
wagoned to your bedside
in a clear, germless glass.

MAY

Lying face up, all the sleepers breathed prayers
in the languages of grasses as they're mown,
or the voice within a peach, the wrinkly kernel,
those dangling lungs that sing in sun-starved orchards
when a flux in the light wakes the bees.

GARDEN WITH NO BOUNDARY

Friend, is this the way to Tenryūji?
There's a rush and clacker of wind in bamboo

and a garden with no boundary.
At the strolling pond, planets cross irises.

Monks have borrowed a mountain
where they let the seasons be.

I will sit among the blossoms of a blown cherry tree
while day, with its heartbeat, comes to nowhere with me.

SENSŌJI

Asakusa Kannon Temple, Tokyo

Around a big brass cauldron, cupping hands,
they throw cedar smoke into their hair to cure their pains.
I do the same. My son's absence goes on
like a breath held years long.

The temple looms, about to fly up on red-gold wings.
Our guide, who knows everything, is the size
of a thorny brushstroke. She scoops a hunk of smoke
rubs it on her cheeks *for mother and for self, for wrinkles and longevity.*

As for me, my Western brain thinks it's midnight.
I ask the Buddha to teach me that it's day.
The guide shakes my elbow. Our group has moved on
to catch a train along the sea—it runs without a human crew.

The world was never yours to lose, she says. *Look around.*
Everywhere a clock. All you have is compassion and time.

SUMI-E

Soon every line can only say obliterate.
Birds, erased W's, wing then wing.
A tide brushes out the lavender wipe by wipe,

Windless August night effaces any rise
that once was—could be—wave.

PICTOGRAPHS

Gray rainbows fanning toward the sea.
Primroses, lightfall. Then
into the blackbird tunnel we slide
and read our maps again.

There's time in every signal.
Your clockface feels my hand.
A hard turn through the mountain,
and we are merely wind.

Once I could track the boundaries
of each migrating dune.
But now each peak seems foreign,
an anthill on the moon.

Dusk is a curl falling to earth.
Cows nod at the onrushing train.
They turn to the sheep who sniff seaweed
and soak up time like rain.

A star's ray cuts through a coal mine,
and cropdust blocks the sky.
Down's up, up's down.
All tunnels lead past day.

Every sign's a sign, my love.
Out of the tunnel we slide.
The sea throws every kind of moon.
Sky reels in every tide.

And every track is through the heart,
and every edge a land.
And all the ospreys in the sun
ink fishhooks in the sand.

IN WINTER WE GO TO HAVE OUR PORTRAITS PAINTED

January and our artist friends
can't draw us fast enough.

There's an elevator in the bedroom, a sick bed
in the studio. A helper holds the dying painter
up by the belt. His wife squeezes blue onto the tray
where she and her husband share paint.

The artists look at us. They look—
as if we were swans eating so much snow,
we go blank when low sun is in the eyes
by the bleached bank of the green pond
beside the greenless trees.

But if they run the brush across the white just right,
perhaps Death will see none of us.

I go right up to your portrait, breathe hard.
Something so lifelike about those gray curls.
"It doesn't look like you." The man pants this out.
The woman, with intense regard at her small canvas,
continues her precise marks for minutes more.
"This doesn't either," she says, looking surprised.

We love these people, and they love us,
but neither one can catch us as we are—
cutting lakes in slow, ruffling rings.

The portraits mutate, unrecognizable
to unrecognizable.

Our friend dies. I lose my watch.
It will take a year to find
in the little drawer next to the bed.

One day we are awake—brush of
lingering blank light; bleached white plumes; eyes
blackened. And you say, "Stay."

ISLAND OF OWLS

Waves beach bodies that shake,
push to crawl. I crawl too,
belly to earth, like a porcupine

dragging toward eel grass.
Have you seen her, I say,
and I do not see.

Have you seen him? I hear.
And everyone is saying—
it is all the birds are saying—

seen her? seen him? Rushes
rippling, new moon
melting, and who

calls, o fog-eyes, is it
who, is it you? Who
will not be lost to us?

The Dead, At Home,

snag on brush and low cactus.
They swing like paper streamers
or like land
          changing hands.
No cure for this, only white gauze rising:
a dry light across a ribbed gash
that floods in spring, driving
the wild goats up onto a knife edge.
Leopards leap up
quietly after them.

          Myself,
I have been occupied,
prayerless in a cave,
reconstructing the temple of Solomon
in the creases of this gray next
mud tunnel room, walls in which wasps
have dug millions of holes,
          the buzz
like living water.

How beautiful the falls of En Gedi.
How lonely the low-slung acacias
on a cliff above the Dead Sea.

Everyone's hideaway
          is on top
of someone else's. Everybody's water
is everyone's wave.

          Swimmer, swimmer,
don't put your eyes where the dead live!
Who speaks the word salt
without every wound in pain?

For the young, wisdom
is a tooth to be filled. a wasp says
as it stings me on the tongue.
                              The dead
remember what they never knew.

A LITTLE PLACE

It is better to live in a little place away from a big place,
where the trees from here are not ladders to there,
but lead to clouds. In the little place nothing lands

but birdshit and seed pods, rabbits run stone paths
dragging kale, and oak leaves tumble slow, slower,
lacy cut-out shadows over anthills.

Phoebes rap on eaves, woodpeckers hack hollows.
They catch every skip and skedaddle in a trill
of some sorry cicada snapped across the belly,

luckless and sacred as a twig tossed on a grave.
We're living in the little place, lucky to be.
We weren't born here. We come from filed-tooth buildings

where plastic bags vulture-up, teeter, soar
to look in on death who sleeps on all the beds,
and lies in black bathtubs arrhythmically thrashing.

It's different here. There's a map, if we can read it.
Lilac, needle mound, drying kelps. Ocean's names
in salt on squishy sands. We settle in, and in.

With so much to talk about, what is there to say?
Hair stands on end when we know another day
is running silken hands across our gooseflesh.

THIS COLD WORLD WE FLED TO

And then it never got warm.
We stay away from everyone
and hurry into woods,
into fresh water with snapping turtles.
Plume-tailed birds
come in for a cooling.

Water seizes us with words we need to send
fast, over tongues, through teeth chattering,

As to the soul, well, where are you, Little Hover?

Heart, among the togue, I worry for you
finning through a forest of hooks.

I look up at the moon, and am dizzy thinking
of craters throwing down toward my eyes
a wild, blank snow.

Or the icebergs an archangel hurls into my half-sleep,
two-hand, over-head heave
and heavy breathing, until the splash
takes my breath and everything I wish for,
even fanfares of green bees
bouncing in green blooms.

But *Oh*, we say. Sun ups, ruddies frost,
and we are creatures
made in the likeness.of the cold.
Cold created them, him and her,
cold shivered them, woman and man,

as if surprise had formed us
in the image of surprise.

Our voices get lost in the winter birds.
At every turn we see shelter in each other.
I feel the lean of birches
through your body's lean on mine.

OUT OF SEASON

You know this one, I said, to some song
you would have preferred not to know.
One of those close summers
when we could only sleep in Maine,
but couldn't get to Maine for weeks.
When we did, the ponds darkened blue, like winter.
The coldest time of year, you said.
An eagle's wings looked like snow on snow,
even though there were months to go.
You didn't believe in insurance for anything.
I was raised on it like oatmeal and smoked fish.
But that year, near sleep, we heard
what knocked like a northern catastrophe
blow the full moon past Dog Island.
The Bears jiggled in tromboning sea.
Crazy-haired mergansers ripsawed
at the fish weir. Up in bed you asked
if it took spit, a harmonium—
anything we had—to placate the wind god.
That was when I promised you
the walls would hold.

COASTAL

Won't be long now till all the rides are done.
The calliope inside your sticky lung,
the scruffy goat who stands upon your tongue
will move along. You'll pause, in a pale sun,
to see a trailing mist, as tents come down,
and the patchy parti-colored suits once strung
against the sea, like pennants blown to sing
of snap and slack, are packed for caravan.
Though wind's about to blast the mist from eyes.
and salt's about to leach the heft from heart,
the coal dust hasn't blackened all the dice.
Come, put a little hand stove in your coat.
These circus carts can wobble toward the port.
A creek still bubbles under thickened ice.

COVE SONG

Into the distance, past the harbor,
follow the stair, or not.
Dissect despair. A raven there
will parse a robin's gut
divining half the ways of blood
until your forehead's hot,
until the air is pearly hair
or grubs in a clay pot.
If ever you see orange-streaked stone,
if ever waves go flat,
then shrink yourself and roll yourself,
two lips upon a tit.
Be lichen on a slick-bark birch,
must on a grounded bat.
If everything's alive with death,
then everything will eat.
A chickadee will seize on you
in a scarce winter nut
and plop the husk where net-winged midges
haze a shifty gate.
You'll open out your deepest breath
in long woes of a flute.
And there you'll shake without your hands.
You'll fly without a root.
An hour to cross a windless pier,
to scoop a wave and wait,
blind in a cone of April stars,
gray salt, and herring milt.
Behind that weed, the moon is red.
You'll beak and swallow it.
More tails will wriggle. Every bird
forgets what it has caught.

FIELD GUIDE TO MERCY

Every time I record that squawk, wind comes up.
The birding app turns off.
Might as well be a tractor's brakes, or a poor pen of pigs
attacked by wolves.

The squawk circles back like a crack in vinyl, an old mouth
coughing a bigger hack. Seven bridges detonate, sky heats.
A flight of crickety flutes, a chorus of peeps, song sparrows,
high-over gulls like outdoor faucets turned and turned.

Flies go up in a bonfire. Stars fall like milk while I sleep.
I'm up at dawn thinking that noise is mercy. And the bird
whose wing-shade brings a season without shadow, that bird
who scared off the Angel of Death—what is that bird's name?

FLOATERS

Among shucked seeds of sunflowers
chopped nubs of slugs,
I know you without your glasses and without mine.

We stare as if seeing horizons deforming,
flats to mountain, bubble-eyed collapses.

We peer through undulations of tree scent,
drowse of smoke-sparks blinking.

The stars are bees thrown farther into night
than any creatures thrown before.

We purify each other's hands with ground-up cedar.
Something sets our hands on fire.

Let's never count minutes again.
Hardly anything holds for longer than lightning.

What lasts floats away, what floats may return.
Day goes dark behind the cinder cone,
at night another ridge begins to burn.

SOULBENDERS TONITE
(At David's Folly)

A shady moon pointed me down to the road
where I heard two guitars ripping out the tomatoes.

I didn't know the song.
Then I knew: Get Lucky.

And through stalks and paddocks,
through horse-kicked barn doors,

past hay bale benches, the claps of the crowd,
my wife dancing almost without moving.

I saw myself, older than I had ever been,
shake to the soar of the horns.

HEADSTAND IN THE RAIN

Legs go up. Rain runs from my mouth
down to my eyes.

If ever I was young and upright, and knew the clouds up close,
I have forgotten.

Earth is my heat and water,
and my head is melting, planted there.

AGAIN

Love
requires no long-term memory,

but moon, tides,
ineluctable pulls,

and the meadow flowers
always

coming back from dropped seeds. . .
There have been lightnings,

or I cannot
remember and that recurrent

not remembering—
the meadows,

meadow flowers—
reminds me you walked,

storm-wet this morning
out from the tall rushes,

daylight
on your hands,

and stripping lupine stems
gone past,

pitched green pods
left and right into the goldenrod.

Following your wrist,
I kept losing track,

then heard seeds
rustle or click to land.

JANUS

To the gate we walk, as out-of-our-time
as air bubbles trapped in volcanic rock.

It's east, you say, pointing west.
How easily one erases to the other.

The god of endings hangs on his hinges,
no right, or left, or wrong.

Rondel With Moles And Mountain

We'll go alone into the darkest part.
The sky's wet rust, the camellia-maze a ruin.

Why should it stop us that our eyes are gone?
This is love's year, and week, and day. A chart

is ink, and ink soon smears. Black wind. The route
all streaks and steams. In these caves, one star makes noon.
We'll go alone into the darkest part.
The sky's wet rust, the camellia-maze a ruin.

With our pink paws, we'll shovel mounds of silt
to tunnel to the shrine of Qingcheng Shan.
Past the long bridge, bleak by the plummy moon,
we'll drink the waterfalls. I'll rub your heart.

We'll go alone into the darkest part.

MNEMOSYNE

That night your hair was full of thread.
I almost forgot your eyes
were tea,
                    gyokuro,
                                        jade dew.
You sat by a cove with your little cup—
salt-clay
                    painted
                                dark blue
like something I could
get back to.

            We played a game,
I packed in my suitcase,
Airedale on an airplane to zebra zoo.

                    Near the end
                    I packed a scintilla.

You kept returning to
                        thirty thimbles of tears.

And then I went again for
all the parts of you
                        and v
                        and double you.

Maybe letters were the last
anyone could say
after a thin-spun day,
after a moon like that
                        going

down like new, a green flash.

And I flash back to you,
             green-wet
             with knotted strings
             and dew,

your hair with salt on the strands,
those lined hands
             tasting of tea.

ACKNOWLEDGMENTS

Thank you to my writing teachers in college and graduate school: Robert Lowell, Robert Fitzgerald, Elizabeth Bishop, Stanley Kunitz, Mark Strand, Carolyn Kizer, and others.

Thank you to Mark Rudman—my Columbia classmate, my co-author and co-translator, my publisher in *Pequod,* and my special friend.

Thank you to poetry workshop leaders from Marvin Bell in 1969 to Lucie Brock-Broido, Joan Houlihan, and David Kirby in the 2010's. Thanks in particular to Tom Daley for his close attention to my poems over the past 15 years.

Thank you to The Poetry Society of the UK and to Judith Palmer for supporting my writing in multiple ways—a prize, a London reading at The Poetry Cafe, a podcast, and a film.

Thank you to Susan Gardner at Red Mountain Press.

And above all, thank you to my wife Rebecca.

AGNI: Meeting You After Chernobyl
The American Journal of Poetry: Near-Sonnet With Homunculus
The Baffler: The Origin of Yet
Barrow Street: Functionary, Motivation [Deluge] (forthcoming)
Beloit Poetry Journal: Janus; Landscape With View Of Lawyer
Columbia Journal Of Literature And Art: Headstand In The Rain
Epiphany: Letter From Berlin
Forklift, Ohio: If I Don't See You
Fulcrum: Pictographs
KROnline on the Kenyon Review website: For An Astronomer's Daughter
Linebreak: Rondel With Moles And Mountain
London Review of Books: Border; Mitte
Magma: May; Morning After
The Massachusetts Review: Song Over Song For My Father
the minnesota review: My Aunt Remembers
The Missouri Review: Drishti
Pequod: Without A Whisper
Per Contra: Febbre A Febbraio
Plume: End of the Century; The Dead, At Home
Poetry Society (UK) Website: After the Calm
Raritan: Again; Coastal; Cove Song;
Spillway: Soulbenders Tonite (At David's Folly)
Third Coast: Aubade; Cityscape
Tupelo Quarterly: Stars That Never Touch The Sea
White Whale Review: A Way To The North